A RELATIONSHIP WITH JESUS-CHRIST

ISBN: 9798654353450

A Publication of Tall Pine Books

|| *tallpinebooks.com*

*Printed in the United States of America

A RELATIONSHIP WITH JESUS-CHRIST

YANN E. V ADJANOHON

Tall Pine

I dedicate this book to the *Holy Spirit*, to my mother, *Dora AKPLO* and *to Stephanie Leon.*

CONTENTS

I was really touched at church on a Sunday night by a missionary's way of teaching and how he let the Holy Spirit use him. The presence of God was evident and real that night; there were many healings and miracles. At the end of the service, I went up to the missionary and asked what had brought him so close with Jesus.

He responded with two things, but this book is about one of them. The first thing he said was, "Seek God's face and not His hand." God's hand is His power, the miracles and healings we may witness. God's face is His presence, God the person. He wanted me to stop seeking miracles and healings and instead to start seeking a relationship with Jesus Christ of Nazareth. It is from our relationship with Jesus that everything flows. The most important thing is not miracles and healings; the most important thing is to have a relationship with the One who *works* miracles and healings.

> One thing I ask from the Lord, this only do I seek: that I may dwell in the house of the Lord all the days of my life, to gaze on the beauty of the Lord and to seek him in his temple. (Psalms 27:4)

Even though he was still alive, David wanted to live in the house of the Lord. While reading this passage I asked myself, "How can we live in the house of the Lord while on earth?" I finally realized to live in the house of the Lord is to have a relationship with Jesus Christ of Nazareth. It was because David lived in the house of the Lord that he was victorious over his enemies, received instructions from God, did His will, and that he was successful in all his ventures.

It was because David had a relationship with God that he was called, "a man after God's own heart." He was one of the Generals of God. Generals of faith all have similar characteristics that I would like to share through this book. These generals in the Bible have succeeded because of their relationship with God.

Jesus answered, "I am the way and the truth and the life. No one comes to the Father except through me." (John 14:6)

After the sacrifice of the cross, the first step in forming a relationship with Jesus is to accept Him as our Savior. Accepting Him allows us to also receive the Holy Spirit. The Holy Spirit has lived with Jesus and no one can teach us, or help us to have a perfect relationship with Jesus, except Him. Our relationship with Jesus can be even more intense than those of the Old Testament generals, because today we have the Holy Spirit.

"But whatever were gains to me I now consider loss for the sake of Christ. What is more, I consider everything a loss because of the surpassing worth of knowing Christ Jesus my Lord, for whose sake I have lost all things. I consider them garbage, that I may gain Christ." (Philippians 3:7-8)

1

TO HAVE A RELATIONSHIP WITH JESUS IS TO GIVE YOUR LIFE TO HIM

We talk about Jesus every day without having a relationship with Him. Talking about someone every day, does not make you close. We can talk about someone every day without even loving them or wanting to include them in our lives. We have a relationship with someone we love, with someone who we see a future with. If we love Jesus, if He is important to us, if we see a future with Him, then we need to have a relationship with Him. The first step in having a relationship with Jesus is to give our life to Him.

Jesus came because He wanted to have a relationship with us and to do so, He had to give His life for us. Jesus died to have a relationship with us. He took the first step.

> "The thief comes only to steal and kill and destroy; I have come that they may have life, and have it to the full." (John 10:10)

The Bible says Jesus came to give us life, and have it to full. If we accept a relationship with Him, we must also surrender our life to Him without holding back.

To give our life to Jesus is to accept Him as the Savior of humanity, to believe He died for us, and rose from the dead on the third day.

To give our life to Jesus is to give up all that excludes Him.

> "Whoever finds their life will lose it, and whoever loses their life for my sake will find it." (Matthew 10:39)

If giving our life to Jesus is the first step to having a relationship with Him then Matthew 10:39 suggests that the relationship with Jesus is necessary for life since there isn't any without Him.

> "I have been crucified with Christ and I no longer live, but Christ lives in me. The life I now live in the body, I live by faith in the Son of God, who loved me and gave himself for me." (Galatians 2:20)

If it's Christ who really lives in us, does He lie when we lie? Does He do evil? Is He a thief? Does He live a life of debauchery? Is He resentful? Is He a mocker?

No.

To give our life to Jesus is to die to ourselves, to die to sins, desires and passions of this world. It is also giving up grudges, pride, jealousy, idolatry and living for Him. We often hear, "I will never forgive you." This saying, for example, is not the words of someone who has given their life to Jesus.

To give our life to Jesus is to be free of ourselves. If we are free, nothing will offend us to the point of taking our joy, our patience, or our peace.

To give our life to Jesus is to have *no way* and to let Jesus have *His way* through us.

When we make a donation, it is not to take it back. Why do we say we gave our old life to Jesus, and then we try to take it back? Why are we interested in what's old?

Think about the role of a garbageman. When he arrives at our house, we give him all of our trash. He takes everything that we do not need, everything that we do not want, and he disposes of it. When he returns the following week, we do not ask him to give us back the empty milk carton we threw out. It wouldn't make sense and we would seem foolish. We act similarly in this way when we say we give our life to Jesus and then when we are told something inappropriate, we react quickly. We become furious or violent and hold grudges against others.

> "But whatever were gains to me I now consider loss for the sake of Christ. What is more, I consider everything a loss because of the surpassing worth of knowing Christ Jesus my Lord, for whose sake I have lost all things. I consider them garbage, that I may gain Christ." (Philippians 3:7-8)

When Paul gave his life to Jesus Christ, he realized that former personal gains, in reality, were losses. He goes on to say he has **lost all things** (he has denied himself) **to gain Christ** (to have a relationship with Christ). Paul is saying in order to have a relationship with Jesus Christ, he has to deny himself.

Have we really given our life to Jesus like Paul? Do we look at past gains as losses, or do we still value them? Have we given up everything to gain Christ, or are we trying to live our old life hoping to do so?

If you are reading this, and you have not given your life to Jesus, it is not too late. Here is the opportunity for you to give Him your life. Just pray this with me:

"Lord Jesus, I give myself to You. I give You my life, my sins, my imperfections, my difficulties. I do not want to live for me anymore, but I want to live for You. Today, I decide to give up everything to have a relationship with You. Help me, please."

THIS IS HOW GIVING MY LIFE TO JESUS WILL CHANGE ME:

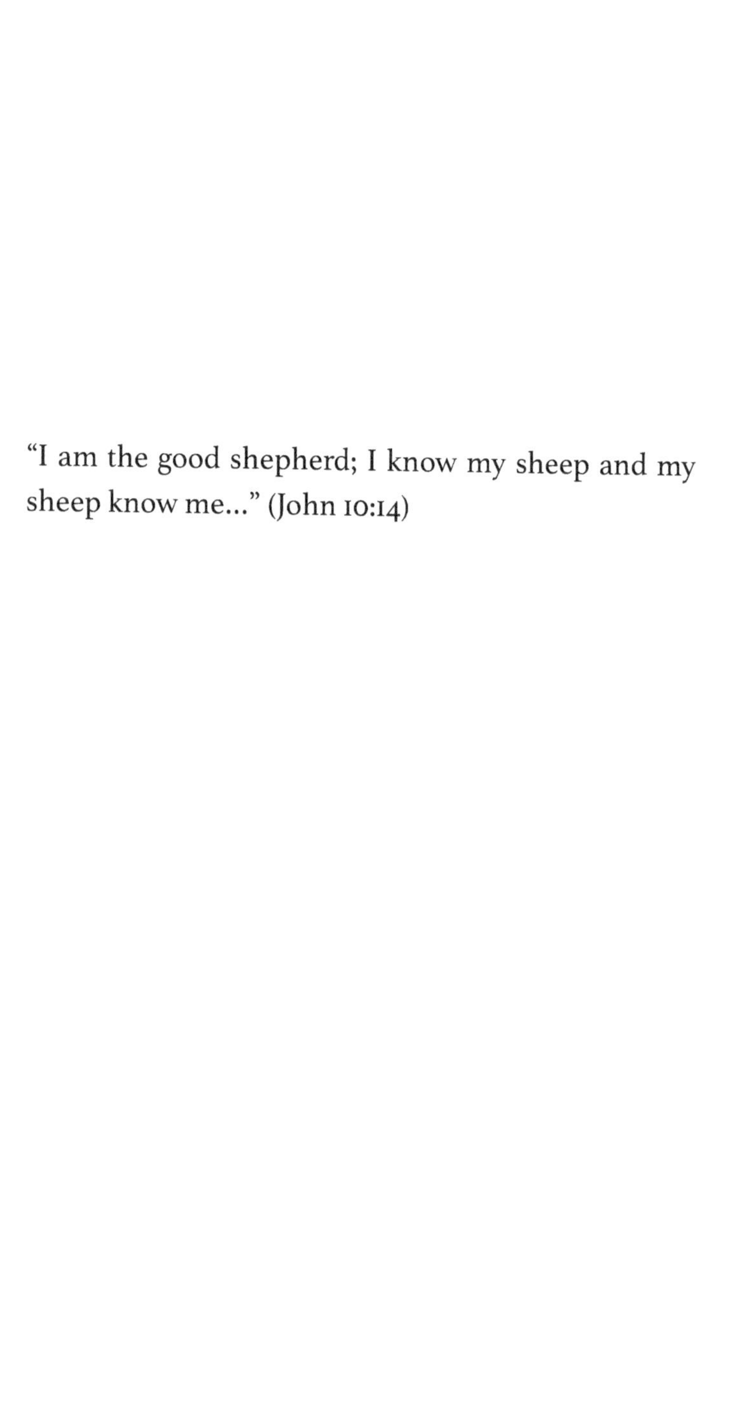

"I am the good shepherd; I know my sheep and my sheep know me..." (John 10:14)

2

TO HAVE A RELATIONSHIP WITH JESUS IS TO LEARN TO KNOW HIM

TODAY, MANY MARRIAGES FAIL BECAUSE THE PEOPLE involved don't know each other. In the same way, we throw ourselves into things that seem attractive without really knowing them, and then we regret the decisions we have made. We give ourselves to sects, social groups, we make alliances with the world of darkness and many other things in search of ephemeral success without knowing the origin or the risks.

Knowing someone is not just about knowing the good parts about them or what they have to offer. It is also about knowing their flaws, their imperfections; who they really are. How do they behave when they are alone or in public? Do they lie? Are they hypocrites? Loyal? How does the lack or the abundance of financial stability affect them? Are they the same in the good or the bad? Are they resentful? Humble? Tolerant? There are so many important questions that need to be answered before engaging in a relationship with anyone.

Jesus does not want us to have a relationship with Him without knowing Him. It would be easier to get involved in a relationship with Him if we know who He is.

It is easy to know Jesus in His word (the Bible):

John 1:1 "In the beginning was the Word, and the Word was with God, and the Word was God."

JESUS CHRIST IS THE WORD OF GOD

"The Word became flesh and made his dwelling among us. We have seen his glory, the glory of the one and only Son, who came from the Father, full of grace and truth." (John 1:14)

JESUS-CHRIST IS GOD

"For God so loved the world that he gave his one and only Son, that whoever believes in him shall not perish but have eternal life." (John 3:16)

JESUS IS THE SON OF GOD

"The Son is the image of the invisible God, the firstborn over all creation." (Colossians 1:15)

JESUS IS THE FIRST BORN OF ALL CREATION

"For God did not send his Son into the world to condemn the world, but to save the world through him." (John 3:17)

JESUS IS OUR SAVIOR

"...that God was reconciling the world to himself in Christ, not counting people's sins against them. And he has committed to us the message of reconciliation." (2 Corinthians 5:19)

JESUS RECONCILES US WITH GOD

"But if we walk in the light, as he is in the light, we have fellowship with one another, and the blood of Jesus, his Son, purifies us from all sin." (1 John 1:7)

JESUS CLEANSES US OF OUR SINS

"And being found in appearance as a man, he humbled himself by becoming obedient to death — even death on a cross!" (Philippians 2:8)

JESUS DIED ON THE CROSS FOR US, TAKING WITH HIM OUR SINS, CURSES AND SICKNESSES

"Jesus answered, "I am the way and the truth and the life. No one comes to the Father except through me." (John 14:6)

"Whoever does not love does not know God, because God is love." (1 John 4:8)

JESUS IS THE WORD, THE WORD IS GOD, THEREFORE JESUS IS GOD AND IF GOD IS LOVE THEN JESUS IS LOVE

> "Love is patient, love is kind. It does not envy, it does not boast, it is not proud. It does not dishonor others, it is not self-seeking, it is not easily angered, it keeps no record of wrongs. Love does not delight in evil but rejoices with the truth. It always protects, always trusts, always hopes, always perseveres. Love never fails. But where there are prophecies, they will cease; where there are tongues, they will be stilled; where there is knowledge, it will pass away." (1 Corinthians 13:4-8)

Let's replace the word love with JESUS and see what we get: **"Jesus is patient, Jesus is kind. He does not envy, He does not boast, He is not proud. He does not dishonor others, He is not self-seeking, He is not easily angered, He keeps no record of wrongs. Jesus does not delight in evil but rejoices with the truth. He always protects, always trusts, always hopes, always perseveres. Jesus never fails. But where there are prophecies, they will cease; where there are tongues, they will be stilled; where there is knowledge, it will pass away."**

Amazing love!

"For to us a child is born, to us a son is given, and the government will be on his shoulders. And he will be called Wonderful Counselor, Mighty God, Everlasting Father, Prince of Peace." (Isaiah 9:6)

JESUS IS WONDERFUL, HE IS A COUNSELOR, HE IS MIGHTY, HE IS A FATHER AND THE PRINCE OF PEACE

"Who then is the one who condemns? No one. Christ Jesus who died—more than that, who was raised to life—is at the right hand of God and is also interceding for us." (Romans 8:34)

JESUS INTERCEDES FOR US BEFORE GOD

"Then one of the elders said to me, 'Do not weep! See, the Lion of the tribe of Judah, the Root of David, has triumphed. He is able to open the scroll and its seven seals.'" (Revelation 5:5)

JESUS IS THE LION OF THE TRIBE OF JUDAH

"The next day John saw Jesus coming toward him and said, 'Look, the Lamb of God, who takes away the sin of the world!'" (John 1:29)

JESUS IS THE LAMB OF GOD

"I am the good shepherd. The good shepherd lays down his life for the sheep." (John 10:11)

JESUS IS THE GOOD SHEPHERD

"Then Jesus declared, 'I am the **bread of life.** Whoever comes to me will never go hungry, and whoever believes in me will never be thirsty.'" (John 6:35)

"Therefore Jesus said again, 'Very truly I tell you, **I am the gate for the sheep.'**" (John 10:7)

"When Jesus spoke again to the people, he said, '**I am the light of the world.** Whoever follows me will never walk in darkness, but will have the light of life.'" (John 8:12)

"...for our "God is a consuming fire." (Hebrews 12:29)

"But because of his great love for us, God, who is rich in mercy..." (Ephesians 2:4)

JESUS IS MERCIFUL

Imagine that, Jesus looked at those who crucified Him, and asked God to forgive them. WOW! Just this act already speaks a lot about the person of Jesus.

Jesus is all we need, when we need Him. He can be a lion, and at the same time a lamb. Jesus is the One we need in the situation we are in. Close your eyes and think about what you want Him to do for you: He has a name for it.

It is not easy to understand this kind of love, but wouldn't you like to have a relationship with a Man of such a character? I promise that you will never be disappointed. No one regrets having a relationship with Jesus. His love is greater than anything man could ever write.

If you want to know Him, read His word and say this prayer with me:

> *"Lord Jesus, I want to know You. You know everything about me. I also want to know everything about You. I want to have a perfect relationship with You. Please let me know more of You."*

THIS IS HOW KNOWING JESUS WILL CHANGE ME:

"One day Jesus was praying in a certain place. When he finished, one of his disciples said to him, 'Lord, teach us to pray, just as John taught his disciples.' He said to them, 'When you pray, say: `Father, hallowed be your name, your kingdom come.'" (Luke 11:1-2)

3

TO HAVE A RELATIONSHIP WITH JESUS IS TO SPEND TIME WITH HIM

IT IS IMPOSSIBLE TO BUILD A RELATIONSHIP WITHOUT spending time with one another. We can't start a relationship with someone we dislike. We want to have a relationship with someone because we like them. When we like someone, spending time together becomes easy and spontaneous.

"We love because He first loved us." (1 John 4:19)

Jesus Christ came because He wanted to have a relationship with us. We can also say that Jesus came to have a relationship with us because He loved us.

By spending time with the people we want to have a relationship with, we are able to know them better. Spending time with Jesus brings forth intimacy, which is essential in any relationship. Intimacy causes us to walk in the same direction with the person we are in relationship with.

It would be hard to have a relationship with Jesus without spending time with Him. A lot of times we hear, "I don't know what to say, I don't know how to pray, I don't know how to start..." When we have a relationship with someone we like, we don't always have words or things to say to them, but the fact that we are spending time together makes us happy and is enough. Being able to enjoy each other's presence satisfies; it should be the same with Jesus. It's okay if we don't know what to say, it's okay if we don't know how to start, but our love for Him should lead us into His presence and His presence is more enjoyable than that of people.

> "You make known to me the path of life; **you will fill me with joy in your presence, with eternal pleasures at your right hand.**" (Psalm 16:11)

Many people think that coming into the presence of Jesus is only to ask Him for things. If we want to build a relationship with someone who just asks us for things, we will have doubts about their love for us and even run away from them. Even though we are only asking Him, Jesus does not run away from us. He wants to have more intimacy with us.

> "One thing I ask from the Lord, this only do I seek: that I may dwell in the house of the Lord all the days of my life, to gaze on the beauty of the Lord and to seek him in his temple." (Psalm 27:4)

David made a request to the Lord, to dwell in His house, to gaze on His beauty, and to seek Him in His temple. David understood that despite his difficulties, despite the problems he had, the only thing that could save him was not the multitude of words, but intimacy with God. He understood that by being in the presence of God, nothing could happen to him, and that his joy was complete in His presence.

> "Whenever the spirit from God came on Saul, David would take up his lyre and play. Then relief would come to Saul; he would feel better, and the evil spirit would leave him." (1 Samuel 16:23)

Saul had an evil spirit that bothered him and to make it leave, he entered the presence of God with David. They did not have to scream and chase evil spirits out because the presence of God brings deliverance and healing.

The disciples of Jesus had seen Him cast out demons, raise the dead, walk on water, and perform many other miracles. Isn't it surprising that they did not ask Jesus to teach them how to perform miracles, how to cast out demons, or even how to raise the dead? Instead, they asked Jesus to *teach* them how to pray. They saw Jesus spending time with God in the morning and at night. They saw Jesus consistently being in the presence of God. They noticed that from that presence came the kingdom of God, and His kingdom brought miracles, deliverance, healings, etc.

> "One day Jesus was praying in a certain place. When he finished, one of his disciples said to him, "Lord, teach us to pray, just as John taught his disciples." (Luke 11:1-2)

*He said to them, "When you pray, say: "'Father, hallowed be your name, **your kingdom come.**"* The kingdom of God comes when we decide to spend time with Jesus.

The more time we spend with Him, the more we become immersed in His nature. We become like Him, we think like Him, we do what He does and what He expects of us.

"When Moses came down from Mount Sinai with the two tablets of the covenant law in his hands, **he was not aware that his face was radiant because he had spoken with the Lord.**" (Exodus 34:29)

"But whenever **he entered the Lord's presence to speak with Him,** he removed the veil until he came out. **And when he came out and told the Israelites what he had been commanded**, they saw that his face was radiant. Then Moses would put the veil back over his face until he went in to speak with the Lord." (Exodus 34:34-35)

Let's look at the life of Moses. The first thing we notice is that he enjoyed spending time with God and that his relationship with Him led him to two things:

1. He received God's instructions for His people and how to lead them.
2. He was immersed with the nature of God.

By spending time with God, His glory has rubbed off on Moses to the point where the people could not look at Moses. Spending time with Jesus will allow us to have divine instructions not only for our lives but also for the people around us. Spending time with God will make us have His nature to the point where the whole world will be able to see in us that Jesus Christ of Nazareth is real. The time spent with Jesus is never lost. We may not feel or hear anything, but every moment spent in His presence makes us more like Him.

After leaving the presence of God, Moses did not know that his face was shining. He finally realized what was happening because of how people reacted towards him. Even if we don't see the effects, or the impact, of time spent in His presence right away, the day will come when we will. On this day, we will be faced with an unusual situation that would have once scared us, but now we will know the exact attitude to have and how to face the problem with assurance and peace. This will be the time to realize that it is the result of the moments we spent in His presence.

> "When the day of Pentecost came, they were all together in one place." (Acts 2:1)

On the day of Pentecost, the lives of those who waited in the upper room changed drastically because they were spending time with Jesus. To spend time with Him transforms us radically and leads us into our destiny.

Spending time with Jesus gives us ease and access to everything. Before their fall, Adam and Eve were permanently in the presence of God. They were immersed with His nature and were on good terms with Him. Their life changed right after they sinned because they came out of that presence. For example, when Adam left the presence of God he lost access to all he had. Genesis 3:19 "By the sweat of your brow you will eat your food until you return to the ground..."

Without Jesus everything becomes harder. Spending time with Him brings us back to the state of Adam and Eve before the fall. Yes, it's possible.

We can also spend time with Jesus by reading His Word. A healthy relationship involves people listening to each other. When we talk to Jesus, He listens to us. We must be able to listen to Him as well when He talks to us. He takes everything we tell Him seriously, and we must equivalently take everything He tells us seriously. God speaks to us in many ways and one of the tools He uses to speak to us is His Word. We must be able to spend time with Him by listening to Him through His Word. If we want to constantly listen to Him, it's easy, we just have to open our Bible and hear Him speak to us. Our time in His Word should not be seen as work, but as moments of joy, transformation, restoration and teaching with Jesus, our bridegroom, the love of our life. All that we have spoken of concerning the presence of God remains true also in reading the Bible.

> "The Spirit gives life; the flesh counts for nothing. **The words I have spoken to you—they are full of the Spirit and life.**" (John 6:63)

The most important thing is that we develop a relationship with Him by reading His word. A relationship cannot be formed without intimacy, and intimacy cannot occur without spending time together. We all need His presence. Let's say this prayer:

> *"Lord Jesus, one thing I ask is that I may dwell in Your house all the days of my life, to gaze on Your beauty and seek You in Your temple. I want to be intimate with You Jesus. Please help me to have a better relationship with You." Amen*

THIS IS HOW SPENDING TIME WITH JESUS WILL CHANGE ME:

"But seek first his kingdom and his righteousness, and all these things will be given to you as well." (Matthew 6:33)

4

TO HAVE A RELATIONSHIP WITH JESUS IS TO MAKE HIM THE PRIORITY

WE PROVE OUR LOVE TO SOMEONE BY MAKING THEM A priority and showing them that they are special. Anyone we choose to prioritize will surely notice it. When we make a person a priority we put them first and everything else comes after them. What comes first in our lives is usually our priority.

What are we spending time on? Who do we spend time with? What do we invest in? What occupies our mind? Struggles? What comes up the most in our conversations? Sex? Money? All of these things can become priorities.

Anointing, miracles, and ministry work can become priorities. To work in ministry does not necessarily mean we are making Jesus our priority. Judas was with Jesus every day, he was in ministry, but his priority was not Jesus. Money had more value to Judas than Jesus. A pastor who speaks only of the growth of his ministry and the power of God, and only makes these things his priority, misses the point.

By making Jesus his priority, he will see the hand of God in his ministry. People suggest that we should focus more on things and situations that are deemed important in the eyes of the world. We are often told that God would have wanted us to worry about this or that. It is a lie. Nothing is more important than Jesus Christ of Nazareth. Work, children, home, money, nothing is more important than Christ. Not making Him our priority can make us idolaters. When we stop making Jesus our priority, we become idolaters because it is no longer about Him but about what he can do for us.

> "But seek first his kingdom and his righteousness, and all these things will be given to you as well." (Matthew 6:33)

Why are we worrying if all things come from Jesus?

> "Can any one of you by worrying add a single hour to your life?" (Matthew 6:27)

We need to understand that Jesus should not be our priority because of what He can do for us; He should be our priority so we may maintain our relationship with Him. In a marriage, both parties make each other their priority not because of selfish desires but because it is important to strengthen and build their relationship.

> "As Jesus and his disciples were on their way, he came to a village where a woman named Martha opened her home to him. She had a sister called Mary, who sat at the Lord's feet listening to what he said. But Martha was distracted by all the preparations that had to be made. She came to him and asked, "Lord, don't you care that my sister has left me to do the work by myself? Tell her to help me!" **"Martha, Martha," the Lord answered, "you are worried and upset about many things, but few things are needed—or indeed only one. Mary has chosen what is better, and it will not be taken away from her.""**
> (Luke 10:38-42)

Martha was taking care of an important matter, but not a priority. Sitting at the feet of Jesus is more important than inviting Him into your house. In other words, having a relationship with Jesus is more important than having religious activities or any other things that involve Him. Jesus is saying that nothing we can do will ever be more important than making Him the priority and having a relationship with Him. WOW! He wanted Martha to understand that He just wanted a relationship with her, and that's what He is telling us now. He wants a relationship with us. Let's not worry about everything else and let's make Jesus our priority.

Making Jesus the priority is:

- To make Him the first in ALL
- To include Him in ALL
- To take interest in what interests Him
- To do what He wants to do
- To love Him more than anything
- To live for Him
- To trust Him
- To look only at Him for ALL

All this is not to say that Jesus does not want us to have priorities, but the most important of all priorities is Jesus Christ of Nazareth. He will position all the other priorities in our lives.

To make Jesus the priority is to have Him in our thoughts, in our mouth, all the days of our lives, to have a better relationship with Him.

Pray with me:

"Lord Jesus, I'm sorry I haven't done a good job at putting You first in my life. If there are things that are idols in my life and I do not realize them, Lord, reveal them to me and remove them. From today on, I make the decision to make You my priority. I only want to think about You, talk about You and live for You. Teach me to make You my priority, please." Amen

THIS IS HOW MAKING JESUS THE PRIORITY WILL CHANGE ME:

"Whoever claims to love God yet hates a brother or sister is a liar. For whoever does not love their brother and sister, whom they have seen, cannot love God, whom they have not seen?" (John 4:20)

"Whoever does not love does not know God, because God is love." (1 John 4:8)

5

TO HAVE A RELATIONSHIP WITH JESUS MEANS TO LOVE OTHERS

IF WE DO NOT HAVE LOVE IN US THEN WE DO NOT HAVE a relationship with Jesus. It is true that we are all different; we do not have the same tastes or desires. My favorite color may be blue and yours may be green, but that shouldn't stop us from being in a relationship. What could stop us from being in a relationship is the way we choose to live our lives.

If one hates nightclubs, alcohol, and drugs, they will not want to have a relationship with someone who loves those things. Even when they decide to risk it and get involved and the other party makes no effort, the relationship cannot last.

Jesus Christ is **love** and He loves us no matter what. We cannot have a relationship with Him if we don't have love in us. It's a lifestyle.

"Jesus replied: 'Love the Lord your God with all your heart and with all your soul and with all your mind.' This is the first and greatest commandment. And the second is like it: 'Love your neighbor as yourself.'" (Matthew 22:37-39)

To love ourselves is to love God. If we do not love ourselves, we cannot love God; if we don't love God, we cannot love others. When we read this, we see that it brings us from one step to another: from the love of God to the love of others. God's love for us makes us love ourselves and self love, leads us to love others. Many live in hatred, bitterness, and slander because they haven't learned to love one another, so they don't love God.

"In fact, this is love for God: to keep his commands. And his commands are not burdensome." (1 John 5:3)

This epistle of John says to love God is to keep His commandments. If in Matthew 22:38 Jesus gives us a commandment, which is to love our neighbor as ourselves, then he who does not love his neighbor clearly does not love God.

"Whoever claims to love God yet hates a brother or sister is a liar. For whoever does not love their brother and sister, whom they have seen, cannot love God, whom they have not seen?" (John 4:20)

If we don't have a good relationship with people, it will be hard to have one with Jesus. The word of God is clear on this.

> "Therefore, if you are offering your gift at the altar and there remember that your brother or sister has something against you, leave your gift there in front of the altar. First go and be reconciled to them; then come and offer your gift." (Matthew 5:23-24)

This shows how important it is for God that we have a good relationship with other people. The gift we offer can be our songs, our worship, our prayers, or our relationship with Jesus. Before we have a relationship with Him it is crucial that we are on good terms with our fellow brothers and sisters.

> "If you love those who love you, what reward will you get? Are not even the tax collectors doing that?" (Matthew 5:46)

To love others is not to love only those who love us, but to love those who don't love us as well.

To love others is to look at them the way Jesus looks at them. The Bible says that God so loved the world that He sent His only Son. Jesus loves Muslims, Jesus loves Buddhists, Jesus loves criminals, Jesus loves everyone. Jesus loved those who crucified Him.

It is this type of love that we are called to. Though there are many people who do not believe in Jesus, He protects them, He watches over them, He provides for them every day. Our love for others must be similar to this. We must be able to help those in need, as much as possible whether they are Christians or not, and whether they like who we are or not.

> "But I tell you, love your enemies and pray for those who persecute you." (Matthew 5:44)

To love others in the ways of Jesus is to repay evil with good; it is to pray for those who persecute us.

To love others is to intercede for them, to bring their names before the throne of God so that God may bless them as we would like to be blessed as well. To love others is to forgive when we are offended; it is to never hold grudges. To love others is to never judge them and not indulge in calumny. To love others is to have a relationship with Jesus.

"And as for you, brothers and sisters, never tire of doing what is good." (2 Thessalonians 3:13)

People will abuse our love, they will take advantage of it, and they will use our love to manipulate us. They will do it until the enemy begins to whisper in our ears saying, "this person thinks you are stupid, they believe you are naive."The enemy will send many other thoughts of this kind, just so that we will stop loving people. We have to understand one thing: we do not love others only because Jesus is asking us to do so, or because we want to have a relationship with Him. We love others because just as Jesus is love, we too become love, and love never fails. May love never become a chore for us so that we get tired of it. Let's *become love* so that nothing people do will stop us from loving them.

"Preach the word; be prepared in season and out of season; correct, rebuke and encourage—with great patience and careful instruction." (2 Timothy 4:2)

To love others is not to only tell them what they want to hear, but to have the courage to tell them when they are doing wrong things, to be able to correct them without humiliating or judging them. When our children misbehave, it is not difficult for us to tell them, because we love them and we don't want to see them suffering the consequences of their misbehavior. Let's have the courage to correct our brothers and sisters in gentleness and in love.

"For the entire law is fulfilled in keeping this one command: 'Love your neighbor as yourself.' If you bite and devour each other, watch out or you will be destroyed by each other. So I say, walk by the Spirit, and you will not gratify the desires of the flesh." (Galatians 5:14-16)

"But the fruit of the Spirit is love, joy, peace, forbearance, kindness, goodness, faithfulness, gentleness and self-control. Against such things there is no law." (Galatians 5:22-23)

Christianity as a whole is all about love so much so that the fruits produced by the Holy Spirit, allow us to love.

- **Love:** we must love one another.
- **Joy:** if we don't have it, it will be difficult to love others and to bring joy to them.
- **Peace:** without peace, how can we love, exhort, encourage, edify or pray for others.
- **Forbearance (Patience):** without it we could not forgive.

- **Kindness:** quality of a good person. It will be impossible to love without kindness.
- **Goodness:** disposition of the heart by which one likes to do good to others. This requires love too.
- **Faithfulness:** doesn't exist without love.
- **Gentleness:** essential to correct or to calm quarrels.
- **Self-control:** without it, it would be easy to hate, to get angry, etc.

The fruits of the Spirit help us to love one another and therefore have a relationship with Jesus.

Pray with me:

"Lord Jesus, You are love, and I want to be like You. I want to be love too. Make love become my nature. Teach me to see my brothers and sisters the way You see them. Fill my heart with love, joy, peace, patience, kindness, goodness, faithfulness, gentleness and self-control, please. I declare that from today on, I love unconditionally." Amen

THIS IS HOW LOVING OTHERS WILL CHANGE ME:

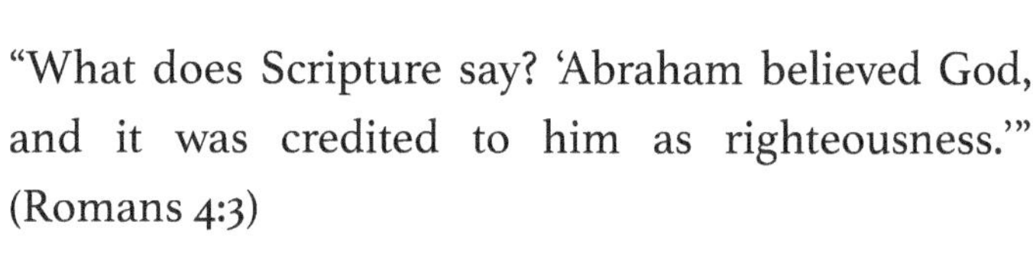

"What does Scripture say? 'Abraham believed God, and it was credited to him as righteousness.'" (Romans 4:3)

6

TO HAVE A RELATIONSHIP WITH JESUS IS TO TRUST HIM

WE OFTEN HEAR THAT IT'S IMPOSSIBLE TO BUILD A relationship without trust. Well, it is impossible to have a relationship with Jesus without trusting Him. Trusting someone is having faith in them, believing in their word. We trust someone we know, it would be unwise to trust a stranger.

We get to know someone by spending time with them and then we decide whether we want to trust them or not.

A child who trusts his parents, puts faith in them. He knows they are faithful. He knows they will provide for his needs and take care of him, therefore he is not worried about anything.

It is easier for us to trust people than to trust God. We also put trust in ourselves, in our so-called abilities. We trust more in what people tell us versus what God tells us. We love Jesus, but not enough to trust Him completely. Trust in people produces imperfect and temporary results, but trust in Jesus produces perfect, lasting results and leads us into our destiny in Christ.

> "Thomas said to him, 'My Lord and my God! Then Jesus told him, "Because you have seen me, you have believed; blessed are those who have not seen and yet have believed.'" (John 20:28-29)

It is easy to trust someone when we can see them. It would be as easy for us to place our trust in Jesus if after rising from the dead, He lived on earth and was seen by all. When Jesus shared His days with Thomas...Thomas had no problem trusting Jesus. When Thomas couldn't see Jesus anymore, it became a problem. A few days later, the trust in Jesus came back when He appeared to Thomas. The fact that Jesus is not visible challenges our intellect, because we've learned that what we don't see doesn't exist. Look around, the air we breathe, the nature that surrounds us, the animals etc...so many things that we see that show the reality of Jesus Christ of

Nazareth. The simple fact that we live is proof of His existence. Jesus is more real than anything, He is more real than our reality, just look around. Let's surrender to Him and we'll see how real He is. As you read this book aren't you able to notice His tangible presence? Jesus says, "...blessed are those who have not seen and yet have believed." They have come to realize that Jesus is real, they understand who He really is and they are able to see Him everywhere. They are blessed because believing in Him, while unable to see Him, makes their relationship perfect .

We trust our cars, our different means of transportation (buses, planes, trains, etc.) even though we don't know what they are made of. If we can trust things that are imperfect, then we can trust Jesus who is perfect. Not trusting Him is also a proof of ingratitude. Not putting our trust in Him, is to forget what He has done for us.

It's easy to say that we trust someone, but saying it is not enough.Trusting Jesus is showing it by our dependence and expectation in Him alone.

"David said to Saul, 'Let no one lose heart on account of this Philistine; your servant will go and fight him.' Saul replied, 'You are not able to go out against this Philistine and fight him; you are only a young man, and he has been a warrior from his youth.'

But David said to Saul, 'Your servant has been keeping his father's sheep. When a lion or a bear came and carried off a sheep from the flock, I went after it, struck it and rescued the sheep from its mouth. When it turned on me, I seized it by its hair, struck it and killed it. Your servant has killed both the lion and the bear; this uncircumcised Philistine will be like one of them, because he has defied the armies of the living God. The Lord who rescued me from the paw of the lion and the paw of the bear will rescue me from the hand of this Philistine."

Saul said to David, 'Go, and the Lord be with you.'" (1 Samuel 17:32-37)

David had a close relationship with God and learned to depend on Him only. He had put his trust in the Lord. Goliath frightened the people of Israel, including King Saul, because of their ingratitude: they forgot what God had done for them before. David was not afraid because he remembered what God had done for him and how He had delivered him repeatedly.

Let's put a focus on the behavior of the people of Israel, Saul, and David, facing a difficulty. We notice that ingratitude produces fear, but recognition leads to assurance and confidence. Faced with our various difficulties we can choose to be afraid or choose to remember the goodness of Jesus in our lives and trust Him. The people of Israel wondered how they were going to destroy Goliath through their human reasoning, but David relied on the Lord, which produced a perfect and lasting result (the death of Goliath) and propelled David into his destiny (to become King).

Often, we decide to trust Jesus in a specific area, but we put Him aside in others. We hear: "Jesus cannot do anything for me in this situation" or "Leave Jesus alone, He did not push you into this." We put Him in a box; it is what we believe that Jesus can do, that He will do for us. We must be able to trust Him in EVERYTHING: our finances, our fears, our uncertainties, our difficulties, and our family. Even if the situation in which we find ourselves in is the result of sin, we can trust Him to rescue us. We must be able to trust Him even at the cost of our lives.

"All these people were still living by faith when they died. They did not receive the things promised; they only saw them and welcomed them from a distance, admitting that they were foreigners and strangers on earth." (Hebrews 11:13)

We don't trust Jesus just because of our material needs. We know that we trust Him when we have faith in Him with or without receiving ALL we have been asking for. Trusting Jesus does not stop with the fulfillment of our prayers, but our trust in Him is perpetual and based on His word. This is what His words say:

> "Keep your lives free from the love of money and be content with what you have, **because God has said, 'Never will I leave you; never will I forsake you.'"** (Hebrews 13:5)

As far as finances are concerned, Jesus promises to be with us. He will not allow us to be destitute. He promises to be there when we need money.

> "...and teaching them to obey everything I have commanded you. **And surely I am with you always, to the very end of the age.**" (Matthew 28:20)

Jesus promises to be with us so that we can fulfill His will. He does not send us without being there with us. Jesus promises that nothing will keep Him away from us. Nothing we can do will make Him run away because He promises to be there every day until the very end of age. Jesus is always present.

> "Come to me, all you who are weary and burdened, **and I will give you rest.**" (Matthew 11:28)

When we are exhausted and cannot handle things anymore, Jesus promises to intervene on our behalf. He promises to allow us to rest while He takes care of the situation.

> "But the Advocate, **the Holy Spirit, whom the Father will send in my name,** will teach you all things and will remind you of everything I have said to you. 27 **Peace I leave with you; my peace I give you.** I do not give to you as the world gives. Do not let your hearts be troubled and do not be afraid." (John 14:26-27)

The Holy Spirit who helps us to live as Jesus, has been promised to ALL to teach us. This Holy Spirit who walked with Jesus and who raised Him is promised to us. Jesus doesn't want us to deal with confusion and panic and He gives us peace.

"And I will do whatever you ask in my name, so that the Father may be glorified in the Son." (John 14:13)

Here is a promise that includes many others. Jesus promises to answer us when we mention His name.

What a promise!

"The one who does what is sinful is of the devil, because the devil has been sinning from the beginning. **The reason the Son of God appeared was to destroy the devil's work."** (1 John 3:8)

Jesus came to destroy sin.

"However, as it is written: 'What no eye has seen, what no ear has heard, and what no human mind has conceived'—**the things God has prepared for those who love him—**" (1 Corinthians 2:9)

Jesus promises us a life filled with pleasant surprises and abundance.

"And these signs will accompany those who believe: In my name they will drive out demons; they will speak in new tongues; they will pick up snakes with their hands; and when they drink deadly poison, it will not hurt them at all; they will place their hands on sick people, and they will get well." (Mark 16:17-18)

Jesus promises us that we will walk in His power.

There are thousands of promises in the Word of Jesus. He is real and He is not a liar. We must be able to grasp His words and trust Him.

Trusting Jesus has nothing to do with laziness and does not encourage people to flee from their responsibilities. For example, when we don't have a job, we don't stay at home waiting for employers to knock on our door. To get the job, we must first choose the field of activity in which we want to work, then submit our application to companies we have selected, and finally we put our trust in Jesus to be hired.

Putting our trust in Jesus requires action. David did not just imagine taking down Goliath by doing nothing. He took the initiative to go fight him and put his trust in Jesus to have victory.

I have a friend named John who called me to tell me that Jesus had asked him to go with me to Benin in West Africa for an evangelistic crusade. John lived in Arizona and I lived in Ohio, two states that are far from each other. The day before we were supposed to leave, John had left Arizona for Ohio because that was where we were departing for Benin. I went to the airport to pick him up and to my surprise John told me he did not have his ticket to Benin.

To hear him say that shocked me and I started asking questions about him when he said to me, "Jesus told me to go with you for the crusade so He will take me. I don't know how, but I know that I will be in Benin with you." I was disturbed by all these words, but at the same time I wanted to see how all this was going to end. John had refused to accompany me back home and wanted to wait at the airport in Ohio.

The next day I saw John at the airport reassuring me to leave in peace and that he will come and join me. I landed in Benin and John still did not have a way to get there. I went to Benin a week before the crusade to help with logistics and the overall organization of the crusade. John and I communicated daily but no news regarding his arrival in Benin. To my surprise, three days before the crusade John called me to tell me that his ticket had been bought and that he would be there.

The next day I went to get him at the airport in Benin. As Jesus had told him, John was indeed at the crusade with me. John put his trust in the word of

Jesus and despite not having the ticket for Benin in time, he still packed his bag and came to Ohio. He demonstrated his confidence in Jesus, who once again showed him His faithfulness.

Trusting Jesus is believing that He is with us and that He will support us in our various projects. Trusting Jesus is to give ourselves to Him, to be in complete submission to His Word, to expect Him for everything and to depend on Him only.

Pray with me :

"Lord Jesus, it is difficult for me to trust You in everything. I know You are not a liar and Your word is true. Help me to believe more in You and in Your word. I don't know how to go about it, but from today on, I want to live my life depending on You. Please help me so that our relationship becomes better. "
Amen

THIS IS HOW TRUSTING JESUS WILL CHANGE ME:

"Therefore go and make disciples of all nations, baptizing them in the name of the Father and of the Son and of the Holy Spirit..." (Matthew 28:19)

7

TO HAVE A RELATIONSHIP WITH JESUS IS TO EVANGELIZE

IN ALL RELATIONSHIPS, WE TRY TO PLEASE EACH OTHER. If one loves flowers, and the other loves perfumes, they will try as much as possible to offer gifts in keeping with each other's desires.

Nobody will see their spouse worried and sad without asking what is troubling them and trying to make them happy.

> "The Lord is not slow in keeping his promise, as some understand slowness. Instead he is patient with you, **not wanting anyone to perish, but everyone to come to repentance.**" (2 Peter 3:9)

Jesus, with whom we seek to have a relationship, weeps over souls who do not know Him. It is sad for

Him to see that those whom He died for, do not benefit from the sacrifice He made on the cross. One of the things that saddens Him even more is when a Christian who is in contact with unbelievers, does not mention Him.

> "A good man brings good things out of the good stored up in his heart, and an evil man brings evil things out of the evil stored up in his heart. **For the mouth speaks what the heart is full of.**" (Luke 6:45)

If we do not speak of Jesus, it is because He does not yet occupy the first place in our hearts. We know how to talk about our problems or projects to anyone who wants to hear them, but when it comes to talking about Jesus, we make it a taboo. We are ashamed or we use the general excuse "I don't know what to say."

Growing up, when our parents would leave the house, they would give us specific instructions. Generally, their last words were the most important. For example, when my parents left, they would tell me not to open the door until they returned. They would ask me to do other things, but the last instruction and what mattered the most to them was to not open the door. When Jesus was going to heaven, He left us one last instruction which is probably very important to Him:

> "Therefore go and make disciples of all nations, baptizing them in the name of the Father and of the Son and of the Holy Spirit…" (Matthew 28:19)

If Jesus speaks of evangelizing last, it's because it has a huge place in His heart and if we want to have a relationship with Him, we will focus on what He is focusing on.

One day I left Columbus for Minnesota, my flight stopped in Chicago and I had to board for my final destination. While boarding, the agent who took my ticket asked me a question: "Could you help in case of emergency?"

I did not understand the question but I answered yes. At the entrance of the plane another agent checks my ticket and asks me the same question "Could you help in an emergency? "

He went on to explain to me that my seat was different. It was a seat in the exit row and happened to have more leg-room. The agent indicated that because of this advantage I should help in the case of an emergency.

My answer was the same. Before taking off, a host approached me to ask me the same question "could you help in case of emergency" my answer was still the same, "yes." At that moment I realized that Jesus was asking me the same question. The exit door represented the wall between the world and Jesus. The fact that I had more space was the fact that God blessed me and gave me grace so that I could be saved and help others. The question Jesus was asking me was, "Can you help my people leave the world to ME, as I have done you the grace? I was deeply touched and my answer was "yes Lord, yes" and He said "**EMERGENCY IS NOW**."

To have a relationship with Jesus is to be able to listen to His heart. His heart is saying it's an emergency to make disciples of all the nations. To evangelize is not only the role of pastors, teachers, prophets, apostles or evangelists; it is the responsibility of all believers.

> "I tell you that in the same way **there will be more rejoicing in heaven over one sinner who repents** than over ninety-nine righteous persons who do not need to repent." (Luke 15:7)

It is so important to evangelize. With each saved soul there is joy in heaven.

Let's not forget what attracted us to Jesus: it's His love. To evangelize is to speak of the love of God manifested through Jesus Christ of Nazareth. We cannot evangelize by calling out flaws, or by claiming to be better, because this is judgment; not winning over souls. Judgment is for God alone. Many remain in the world because they do not know love. They cannot imagine being loved and when sharing with them the love of Jesus, the forgiveness of sins by His blood and His plan for their lives, hope is reborn in them and they fall in love with this Jesus we are speaking of. Judging them and treating them like everyone else, will make them run away. Let's remember that we are saved not because we are perfect but because of the grace of God. Jesus brought us to Him so that we could bring others as well.

Evangelizing is not to argue. When we evangelize, we don't try to convince, that's the role of the Holy Spirit. Our role is to talk about the love of Jesus and plant a seed. If we are positively received, we will continue to be led by the Holy Spirit. Otherwise, it would be better not to engage in human reasoning, the planted seed will produce fruit in due season.

To set a good example is an effective way to evangelize. People are good observers. Whether in our workplace, in our family, in the street, or even in church we are observed. If we live like the world, we will not have done anything extraordinary. Living with a relationship with Jesus will draw others to us with questions, and then it will become easy to present Jesus Christ of Nazareth.

> "My message and my preaching were not with wise and persuasive words, but with a demonstration of the Spirit's power, so that your faith might not rest on human wisdom, but on God's power." (1 Corinthians 2:4-5)

Several Times in the word of God, some men and women have accepted Jesus after He has performed a miracle or delivered them. Miracles, healings and deliverance are not more important than Jesus, but they are part of His nature. Jesus does this to show His love and His love leads to repentance (Romans 2:4).

By having a relationship with Jesus, we receive His nature so miracles, signs and wonders also become our nature. We must be able to evangelize by manifesting the love of Jesus through His power while acknowledging that we have nothing to do with it and that all the glory goes back to Him.

On our way back from church in Benin, West Africa in the city of Cotonou, on a Sunday, I noticed a crowd of people. I wanted to know what happened, and then I saw a body covered on the ground. I was with my father, a friend, and a member of my staff. We went down to pray for this man because we believed that we serve a miracle-working God. The body was the body of an older man hit by a car. There were about thirty people around us and after a few minutes in prayer I felt that it was a good opportunity to present Jesus Christ of Nazareth.

I talked to those around me, and to my surprise all who were present received the Lord that day. Right after that, the missionary found out that the heart of the man on the ground began to beat, which we did not notice at first. A doctor came and said it was the last beating of his heart and he could not live anymore. He did not come back to life but we believe that a great miracle happened: the man on the ground also gave his life to Jesus and that was the reason we felt his heart beat. If we had not done so, these people would have continued to live their lives far from God, and the man could have died without giving his life to Jesus. The greatest miracle is a soul saved for Jesus Christ of Nazareth.

Funding God's work is important for evangelism. Crusades or evangelical missions require financial resources and support. By donating and helping with financial resources we become evangelists.

However, we shouldn't let this be our only way to evangelize.

> "If you declare with your mouth, 'Jesus is Lord,' **and believe in your heart that God raised him from the dead, you will be saved.**" (Romans 10:9)

To evangelize is not collecting confessions from thousands of people. Many Christians, while evangelizing, don't think about souls but rather focus on how to make them say a prayer. The purpose of evangelism is not to try making everyone repeat after you, but to bring souls to the Lord. To evangelize is to depopulate hell and overpopulate heaven.

Confessing AND BELIEVING save, not just confession. Let's evangelize to bring back *hearts* to Jesus, taking our time, listening and sowing love. Evangelism isn't only effective in crusades, it is also effective when you talk to people one-on-one. During crusades we don't preach as if we were talking to a crowd, but we are preaching for one person at a time, keeping in mind that there will be more joy in heaven for one sinner who repents. This is what makes the heart of Jesus happy.

When we build our relationship with Jesus, we won't be able to see what He puts in us if we are not ready to move for Him. By taking the initiative to evangelize, we will know that we have the gift of prophecy or healing, etc. The more we evangelize, the more we are able to see the nature of God manifested through us because it comes from the relationship with Jesus. Don't overthink it, and go make disciples of all the nations!

Pray with me:

"Jesus, I know you want to see those for whom you came, come to you. I recognize that I was not an effective instrument when I had the opportunity and for that I am sorry. Help me to turn all nations into disciples. Help me to bring joy into heaven. Give me courage, assurance, compassion and equip me with all of Your gifts so I can do this. From today on I want to be useful for You. " AMEN.

THIS IS HOW EVANGELIZING THE GOSPEL WILL CHANGE ME:

Noah had a relationship with God, and because of it his family was spared during the flood.

> "Then the Lord said, 'Shall I hide from Abraham what I am about to do?'" (Genesis 18:17)

God did not hide anything from Abraham because they had a great relationship.

> "...and through your offspring all nations on earth will be blessed,because you have obeyed me." (Genesis 22:18)

Abraham's relationship with God was beneficial to him, but also for us. Our relationship with God can benefit others.

David had a close relationship with God, he killed Goliath, he was made king over Israel and he was called a man after God's heart.

> "Then Peter said, 'Silver or gold I do not have, but what I do have I give you. In the name of Jesus Christ of Nazareth, walk.'" (Acts 3:6)

The relationship the disciples had with Jesus brought forth His nature and they could do what they had seen Him do before. Miracles, signs and wonders accompanied them.

> "Then the man and his wife heard the sound of the Lord God as he was walking in the garden in the cool of the day, and they hid from the Lord God among the trees of the garden. But the Lord God called to the man, 'Where are you?' He answered, 'I heard you in the garden, and I was afraid because I was naked; so I hid.'" (Genesis 3:8-10)

When Adam and Eve disconnected from their relationship with God they had difficult days. They were used to spending time with Him. Adam and Eve lost their relationship with God and began to turn away from Him. They turned away because they realized they didn't have His nature even though they still loved Him.

While they had an excellent relationship with God, they didn't know they were naked because with Him we are like Him, but far from Him we are exposed to the world. We were sinners before our relationship with Jesus Christ, now that we are saved, our relationship with Him makes us live in His Grace where our faults, our iniquities are completely erased and we have a pure conscience to act with confidence and boldness.

Without the relationship with Jesus, we are tormented by guilt, and with a sinful conscience it becomes easier to run away from Him. The more we seek a relationship with Jesus, the more we can hear Him and see Him come to us. His presence becomes real and we get His nature. In the same way, the further away we are from Him, the less we will be able to hear Him and the more we will be aware of this sinful nature. Let's take the example of Judas, the one who betrayed Jesus. Cut off from the relationship with Him and disturbed by his actions (betraying Jesus) he ends up taking his life (hiding away from God).

It is possible to know if we have a relationship with Jesus or not, by the way we choose to live. The relationship with Jesus Christ of Nazareth is necessary, and what we are is only the result of that relationship. A fish cannot live out of water because that's the environment which created it. An uprooted tree cannot grow because the earth is the environment that created it. Similarly, we cannot grow without a relationship with Jesus because we were created by Him. **Jesus living on earth taught us how to have a relationship with Him through the relationship He had with God:**

1. **Jesus gave His life to God.** Jesus gave His life by giving Himself so we can be reconnected to God.

2. **JESUS knew God.** Jesus always spoke of God and His Kingdom to His disciples.

3. **JESUS spent time with God.** *"One of those days Jesus went out to a mountainside to pray, and spent the night praying to God." (Luke 6:12)* Jesus spent most of His time alone with God.

4. **JESUS made God His priority.** *"By myself I can do nothing; I judge only as I hear, and my judgment is just, for **I seek not to please myself but him who sent me.**" (John 5:30)* Everything Jesus did was for God.

5. **JESUS loved others.** *"As the Father has loved me, so have I loved you. Now remain in my love." (John 15:9)* There is no doubt that JESUS had love for those around him. He prayed for those who crucified Him. He died not only for them but for us as well.

6. **JESUS had trust in God.** *"The one who sent me is with me; he has not left me alone, for I always do what pleases him." (John 8:29)*

7. **JESUS evangelized.** *"The one who sent me is with me; he has not left me alone, for I always do what pleases him." (John 14:6)*

Jesus was already teaching us how to evangelize.

If we want to be like Jesus, we must be able to do as He does. We must seek to be like Him by having a relationship with Him, as He had with God. All who could do the will of God are those who have maintained a relationship with Him and all the characteristics that Jesus had are in each of them.

Whatever our field of work is, we have been created to do the will of God. This cannot be done without our relationship with Jesus Christ. The relationship with Jesus is not the guarantee that we will not encounter difficulties. On the contrary, we will, but, because of that relationship, they will be easy to face because we will be able to look at them the way Jesus looked at them.

> "Then the man and his wife heard the sound of the Lord God as he was walking in the garden in the cool of the day, and they hid from the Lord God among the trees of the garden. **But the Lord God called to the man, 'Where are you?'"**
> (Genesis 3:8-9)

After the fall of Adam and Eve, God comes and asks where they are. God is omnipresent, omnipotent and omniscient, He knows and sees everything and is everywhere. Was He not able to know where Adam and Eve were? Of course. Yes! But in his question was another, and God is asking us the same question today. God was asking them, **"Where are you with your relationship with Me?"**

We must be able to answer this question. Have we really given our life to Jesus? Do we know Him? Do we spend time with Him? Do we make Him our priority? Do we love others? Do we trust Jesus? Do we make disciples of all nations?

The relationship with Jesus is essential to do the will of God in our life and others. May God help us in the name of Jesus Christ of Nazareth.

THIS IS HOW A RELATIONSHIP WITH JESUS-CHRIST WILL CHANGE ME:

ABOUT THE AUTHOR

YANN E. V ADJANOHON was Born in New York, then raised in Benin, West Africa. His mother did everything she could to show him the ways of the Lord, but it's only after coming back to the USA for his studies that he gave his life to Jesus Christ and it's since been an ever-growing love story. Yann is an evangelist and the founder of Word Daily Bread, an organization focusing mainly on evangelism through crusades around the world but who also wants to plant churches and show unconditional love to prisoners, orphans widows and the needy. Yann is a father of 2, Emmanuel and Lillian.